THE HOLLOW ESTABLISHMENT

Reflections on Authority, Privilege and the Erosion of Trust

By

Peter Scraton

Dedication

This book is dedicated, first and always, to my children — **Thomas, Jessie and Lottie**. They continue to make me proud in so many ways that matter far more than anything written in this book. Their support, resilience and generosity of spirit give meaning to my work and remind me daily of what truly matters.

I owe a special debt to my closest friend, **Tony Hall**. His intellect, judgement and big brain have shaped many of the conversations from which these essays emerged. His capacity to see patterns, challenge assumptions and connect ideas has been a constant source of inspiration. If this book has coherence, it owes much to his influence.

I also write in gratitude to my parents, **Jean and Brian Scraton**, who are no longer with us. They sacrificed greatly to ensure that my sisters and I were given opportunity, stability and a great start in life. Their modest demeanours and values continue to shape how I see the world. Whatever clarity these pages contain rests on foundations they laid.

This book is also written in memory of my late wife, **Michelle**, who died far too young in 2020. Her kindness, her immense heart and her irrepressible love of life left an imprint on everyone who knew her.

She remains an example to us all of how generosity, courage and joy can coexist, even in difficult times.

And finally, to **Betsy**, my Springer Spaniel and constant companion of the past seven years. Her loyalty and unconditional love have grounded me more than anyone could ever know. She has taken care of me through moments of grief, reflection and renewal. Without her, the world would be a far harder place to navigate.

Acknowledgments

A special note of thanks to Sarah Zayn for her thoughtful editorial guidance, patience, and dedication throughout this book. I am equally grateful to Youha Ashford, Publishing Manager, for her professionalism and support in bringing this project together.

About the Author

Peter Scraton is a senior HR and operations professional with extensive experience across UK and international organisations, supporting large and complex workforces in both commercial and regulated environments. He writes on leadership, governance, economic policy, and sport, with a particular focus on legitimacy, accountability, and the risks posed when ruling elites become detached from the communities and institutions they serve. His work explores how power is exercised, how trust is sustained or eroded, and why effective leadership depends as much on moral authority as formal position. Originally from Tyneside, he now lives in Buckinghamshire.

Epigraph

"The measure of a civilisation is not how it rewards power, but how it restrains it."

— adapted from classical sources

Contents

Introduction – The Age of Exemption

Institutions do not collapse when they are criticised.

They collapse when they begin to defend the indefensible.

Over the past decade, public life has become louder, angrier and more volatile. Elections shock. Scandals accumulate. Institutions defend themselves with ever greater urgency. Populism is blamed. Technology is blamed. Social media is blamed.

The diagnosis is almost always external.

The deeper cause is internal.

Across politics, business, sport and public administration, a single pattern has repeated itself with unsettling consistency: those at the top begin to behave as though the rules apply differently to them. Not illegally, not always corruptly — but asymmetrically. Judgement is softened by proximity. Process replaces accountability. Reputation becomes a shield.

This is how systems hollow.

Authority does not erode because citizens demand too much. It erodes because elites tolerate too much — from themselves and from each other.

The argument of this book is simple and structural:

Legitimacy drains when exemption rises.

This is not a partisan claim. It is not a cultural lament. It is a behavioural observation grounded in history. The Roman Republic did not fail because it lacked laws. It failed because those entrusted with power bent those laws without consequence. The Ancien Régime did not fall because it governed; it fell because privilege detached from responsibility. Modern democracies are not immune to this pattern. They are simply subtler in how it unfolds.

What we are witnessing today is not institutional collapse. It is institutional defensiveness — a quieter and more dangerous condition.

When an error occurs, systems respond with legal containment.

When scrutiny intensifies, they manage optics.

When trust falters, they blame misunderstanding.

The surface remains intact. The interior thins.

This book traces that thinning across contemporary life — from corporate boardrooms to constitutional monarchies, from football governance to presidential conduct. The subjects differ. The pattern does not.

I call it **The Hollowing Cycle**:

1.   Status buffers scrutiny.

2.   Institutions protect proximity.

3.   Process replaces moral judgement.

4.   Accountability becomes selective.

5.   Public trust withdraws.

At first, the withdrawal is quiet.

Then it becomes political.

Then it becomes destabilising.

Populism, in this framing, is not the disease. It is the fever — a symptom of systems that have mistaken insulation for stability.

The public will forgive failure. It will not forgive asymmetry.

The crisis of our time is not that authority exists. It is that authority too often exempts itself from the standards it imposes on others.

Democracies do not require perfect leaders. They require credible restraint.

Where restraint weakens, legitimacy follows.

Where legitimacy thins, stability becomes performative.

This book is not a manifesto. It proposes no sweeping constitutional redesign. Its claim is narrower and more demanding: that the survival of institutions depends less on structural reform than on behavioural symmetry.

Power must be exercised under the same standards it enforces.

When that symmetry is restored, authority strengthens.

When it is not, decline accelerates — quietly, predictably, and then all at once.

SECTION I

POWER WITHOUT RESPONSIBILITY

When privilege detaches from consequence, legitimacy begins to die.

1. When the Rules Stop Applying

History rarely announces its turning points. It leaves traces instead—patterns of behaviour that repeat quietly until they can no longer be ignored. One of the most reliable of those patterns is this: societies weaken not when authority is challenged, but when those who hold authority cease to believe the rules apply to them.

This is not a claim about ideology, nor a lament for a lost moral age. It is an observation grounded in history and visible again today. Across different political systems, cultures and centuries, legitimacy erodes when power becomes insulated, defensive and self-referential.

Recent controversies have made this dynamic difficult to avoid. The continuing aftershocks of the Epstein case, the reputational damage surrounding it, and the norm-breaking Trump presidency are not identical phenomena. They differ in scale, context and consequence. What unites them is not scandal but symbolism: the perception that status alters accountability.

That perception is fatal to trust.

History suggests that legitimacy depends less on perfection than on symmetry. Citizens tolerate error when they believe it is shared, acknowledged and corrected. They become alienated when an error appears cushioned by position. Rules that bend upward corrode authority far more effectively than rules imposed downward.

The late Roman Republic did not collapse because its citizens became unruly. It weakened because elite office-holders increasingly treated public authority as a private entitlement. Patronage networks flourished, corruption was normalised, and accountability became selective. By the time external pressures mounted, civic belief in the *res publica* had already thinned.

The same pattern appeared in early modern France. The Ancien Régime did not fall simply because bread was scarce, but because privilege detached itself from responsibility. Exemptions multiplied. Burdens were asymmetrical. Versailles became not just a palace, but a symbol of elite insulation. When legitimacy evaporates, force and rhetoric are poor substitutes.

Modern democracies are not immune to this logic. They rely less on coercion than on consent, and consent depends on the belief that authority is exercised fairly. When that belief weakens, systems do not immediately collapse. They hollow out.

The danger, then, is not scandal itself. Democracies can survive scandal. The danger is the institutional reflex that follows: defensiveness, delay, legalism without moral clarity. Each instance may appear manageable. Accumulated, they become corrosive.

The central argument of this book begins here. The gravest political risk facing liberal societies today is not populism, polarisation or technological disruption in isolation. It is the slow normalisation of elite exception-making—and the quiet withdrawal of public trust that follows.

Case Study: Enron and Elite Exception-Making

The collapse of Enron in 2001 remains one of the clearest modern examples of power exercised without responsibility. At its peak, Enron was celebrated as an innovative, elite corporation whose executives were treated as visionaries rather than stewards. Internally, complex financial structures were used not to create value, but to obscure risk and protect senior figures from scrutiny.

What made Enron corrosive was not simply fraud, but selective accountability. Executives retained bonuses while losses were hidden; auditors and regulators deferred to reputation; dissenting voices were marginalised. Rules existed, but they did not apply symmetrically.

When Enron collapsed, over 20,000 employees lost their jobs and pensions, while senior leaders had already insulated themselves financially. The damage to trust extended far beyond the firm, contributing to a broader crisis of confidence in corporate governance and financial oversight.

Enron illustrates a central theme of this section: legitimacy collapses when elites assume immunity. Systems do not fail because rules are absent, but because those at the top believe they are exempt from them.

Reference: McLean, B. & Elkind, P. The Smartest Guys in the Room (2003)

2. Epstein and the Architecture of Impunity

The enduring significance of the Epstein affair lies not in shock value but in structure. Crimes were committed, victims harmed, and justice pursued unevenly. That much is no longer disputed. What continues to disturb public confidence is how the system behaved around those facts.

Prosecutorial decisions, plea arrangements, delayed scrutiny and elite proximity created an impression—fair or not in every detail— that accountability was negotiable. The legal system appeared procedurally intact yet substantively compromised. Process functioned; confidence did not.

This distinction matters. Legitimacy is not sustained by procedural correctness alone. It rests on outcomes that align with public expectations of fairness. When a process produces results that appear asymmetrical, trust erodes even if the rules were technically followed.

Institutional actors often respond to such criticism by defending the integrity of the process. That response is understandable and insufficient. Citizens are not wrong to ask whether equal treatment is being delivered, not merely whether boxes were ticked.

History offers parallels. In late imperial Rome, legal forms remained sophisticated even as outcomes favoured the powerful. Law persisted; justice thinned. Tacitus captured the danger succinctly: corruption does not destroy institutions immediately—it hollows belief in them.

The Epstein case has become a modern reference point because it reinforced a suspicion already present: that wealth and access alter how systems respond. Whether that suspicion is universally justified matters less than the fact that it is widely held. Trust, once lost, is not easily restored by explanation.

What emerges is not conspiracy but cynicism. And cynicism is politically potent.

Micro-Case: Teapot Dome Scandal

The Teapot Dome scandal of the 1920s exposed how elite proximity distorts accountability. U.S. Interior Secretary Albert Fall secretly leased federal oil reserves to private companies without competitive bidding. The wrongdoing was not a technical failure but an assumed exemption: Fall behaved as though public assets were discretionary.

The scandal shattered confidence in federal governance and led to the first imprisonment of a U.S. cabinet member. Its significance lies not in punishment but precedent. It demonstrated that legitimacy collapses when senior figures treat authority as entitlement rather than obligation.

Teapot Dome remains an early illustration of a recurring truth: corruption flourishes not where rules are absent, but where elites believe they apply selectively.

3. Symbolic Damage: Andrew Mountbatten-Windsor and Institutional Defensiveness

Constitutional systems rely on symbolism as much as structure. This is particularly true of monarchies, whose authority is sustained by consent, tradition and restraint rather than direct power.

The damage associated with Andrew Mountbatten-Windsor was never confined to the individual. It spread because of how the institution responded. Public concern centred less on legal outcomes than on judgement, accountability and tone. Defensive instincts appeared to outweigh moral clarity. Explanations substituted for acknowledgement.

In such contexts, institutions often underestimate the power of symbolism. They focus on formal limits of responsibility while overlooking reputational consequences. Yet legitimacy in constitutional systems is cumulative. It depends on an assumption of standards higher than mere compliance.

The past suggests that symbolic failures linger. When institutions appear to shield rather than scrutinise those close to power, confidence erodes beyond the immediate case. The public does not parse internal distinctions carefully. It draws conclusions about culture.

This is not a demand for perfection. It is a demand for symmetry. Where symbolism and accountability diverge, authority weakens.

The Withdrawal of Legitimacy: Andrew Mountbatten - Windsor

For decades, Prince Andrew operated within one of the most insulated structures in British public life. His authority derived from position — royal status, military patronage and institutional proximity — rather than electoral mandate or executive delivery. For many years, that was sufficient.

Legitimacy, however, is not permanently inherited. It is sustained through judgement, restraint and alignment with institutional expectations. As public confidence in those qualities weakened, formal rank proved increasingly fragile.

The 2019 Newsnight interview marked a decisive inflection point. Titles were not constitutionally erased, yet public consent was effectively withdrawn. Military affiliations were relinquished. Patronages removed. Official duties ceased. Institutional distance replaced institutional protection.

What shifted was not hierarchy but legitimacy.

This episode illustrates a structural principle: positional authority can absorb reputational strain for extended periods, but once moral credibility fractures visibly, decline accelerates. The protection of office cannot compensate for erosion of consent.

The consequences extend beyond reputation. Role contracts. Influence narrows. Historical memory reclassifies the individual from contributor to cautionary example.

This is not primarily a constitutional story. It is a legitimacy story. Authority borrowed from an institution remains contingent upon sustained credibility. When the social contract weakens, hierarchy offers limited defence. The individual stands exposed once the institutional shield is withdrawn.

4. Norms Are the System: Trump and Democratic Decay

Donald Trump's two terms as President of the USA demonstrate how democratic systems can be strained without formal rupture. Laws remained largely intact. Elections were held. Courts functioned. And yet something fundamental shifted.

The shift lay in norms.

By treating convention as optional, accountability as persecution and personal loyalty as virtue, Trump exposed a truth long understood by political theorists: democracies rely on restraint as much as law. Informal rules—respect for institutions, acceptance of limits, good-faith conduct—are not decorative. They are load-bearing.

Once norm-breaking becomes performative, it invites imitation. What was once unthinkable becomes contestable; what was contestable becomes routine. Institutions struggle not because they are overthrown, but because they are drained of moral authority.

History again provides warnings. Weimar Germany did not fall solely because of the economic crisis. It faltered because elites misused democratic mechanisms, undermined norms and treated institutions instrumentally. Legal forms survived longer than legitimacy.

Trump's current legacy is not singular. It revealed how fragile democratic guardrails become when leaders test them relentlessly. The lesson is not partisan. It is structural.

Micro-Case: Watergate Scandal

Watergate was not primarily a crime of burglary, but of norm erosion. The Nixon administration used executive power to obstruct investigation, intimidate institutions, and frame accountability as disloyalty.

The constitutional system ultimately held, but only because courts, Congress and the press acted independently. What failed first were informal restraints.

Watergate confirms a central lesson: democratic systems survive not because leaders obey the law, but because they respect limits they are not forced to observe. Once norm-breaking becomes strategic, institutions weaken long before laws fail.

5. Why Elite Misconduct Radicalises the Centre

Populism is often treated as a pathology—a deviation from rational politics driven by emotion or ignorance. This diagnosis flatters elites and misreads history.

Public anger tends to radicalise when it encounters asymmetry. When citizens believe that standards are applied unevenly, moderation loses credibility. Trust drains not toward extremism immediately, but toward disengagement, cynicism and then alternatives.

Elite misconduct accelerates this process. Not because the public expects virtue, but because it expects fairness. When that expectation is violated repeatedly, anger becomes rational before it becomes dangerous.

History shows that revolutions are rarely ignited by the most marginalised alone. They gain momentum when the centre concludes that the system no longer merits loyalty. That is the real danger of selective accountability: it alienates those with the most to lose from instability.

The irony is that elites often respond to this anger with moralising language. They warn of populism while ignoring its causes. In doing so, they reinforce the very dynamic they fear.

The lesson of this section is therefore simple and severe. Authority is not undermined primarily by those who challenge it from below. It is undermined when those who hold it treat it as insulation rather than an obligation.

That is where decline begins—not with revolt, but with exemption.

SECTION II

INSTITUTIONS UNDER STRAIN

Systems rarely collapse outright — they hollow out first.

6. VAR and the Crisis of System Trust

Few recent controversies illustrate institutional strain more clearly than the debate around VAR in football. Superficially, the argument appears technical: accuracy versus flow, technology versus tradition. In reality, it is about trust.

VAR was introduced to correct obvious errors and support referees in a faster, more scrutinised game. Its existence is not the problem. Modern sport, like modern governance, cannot simply opt out of technology. The deeper issue lies in how the system is designed, communicated and defended.

VAR's failures have rarely been about technology malfunctioning. They have been about **processes that feel opaque, inconsistent and insulated from consequence**. Decisions appear arbitrary, not because they are random, but because the logic behind them is poorly explained and unevenly applied. When supporters see similar incidents judged differently week to week, confidence collapses.

This mirrors a wider institutional problem. Systems designed to enhance fairness can end up eroding it if they prioritise procedural defensibility over legitimacy. VAR officials can demonstrate that protocols were followed; fans remain unconvinced that justice was done.

The lesson is not that systems should abandon process, but that **process without consent is brittle**. Legitimacy requires transparency, accountability and a willingness to admit error. Where systems appear to protect themselves rather than correct themselves, trust drains away.

VAR has become a proxy for a broader frustration: institutions that insist they are right, while failing to persuade those they govern.

Micro-Case: NHS England Waiting Targets

NHS waiting-time targets were introduced to improve patient care through transparency and accountability. Over time, pressure to meet metrics distorted behaviour. Performance was managed rather than improved; reporting compliance replaced lived experience.

Clinicians understood the gap. Patients felt it. The system could demonstrate adherence to process while trust quietly eroded.

This mirrors the VAR problem precisely: technical systems designed to enhance fairness can undermine legitimacy when outcomes feel disconnected from common sense. Process compliance is not the same as justice perceived.

7. In Defence of Referees: Scapegoating the Visible

One of the quiet injustices of institutional failure is how responsibility is displaced. When systems struggle, they often punish the most visible actors rather than the structures that constrain them.

In football, referees have become lightning rods. Every controversial decision is dissected, slowed down and moralised. Abuse follows. The assumption is that poor outcomes must reflect individual incompetence or bias.

This is rarely true.

Referees operate within frameworks defined by governing bodies: laws of the game, interpretations, performance metrics, technological overlays and public expectations. They are constrained actors, not sovereign ones. When VAR intervenes clumsily, it is the referee who absorbs the anger, not the system that mandated the intervention.

This dynamic is familiar across institutions. Frontline professionals—teachers, doctors, civil servants, regulators—absorb public frustration generated by decisions they did not design. Elites and system architects remain insulated, while visibility attracts blame.

Scapegoating has two consequences. It demoralises those doing the work, and it prevents genuine reform. By personalising failure, institutions avoid confronting structural flaws.

History shows that systems which sacrifice their intermediaries to protect the centre eventually hollow themselves out. Trust cannot be rebuilt by blaming individuals for systemic weaknesses.

8. Regulation Without Authority: When Oversight Loses Credibility

Regulation is meant to reassure the public that complex systems are being governed in the public interest. When regulators lose authority, confidence in the entire system weakens.

Recent debates around utilities, infrastructure and public services reveal a common concern: **regulators appear closer to the organisations they oversee than to the citizens they protect**. Technical competence remains high. Moral authority does not.

This is not usually the result of corruption. It emerges from proximity, professional culture and shared assumptions. Regulators speak the language of the regulated. Over time, enforcement becomes cautious, incremental and defensive. Failure is managed rather than confronted.

The public notices.

When regulatory responses to failure appear slow, legalistic or deferential, trust evaporates. Citizens do not expect perfection, but they expect visible alignment with their interests. When fines are absorbed as costs of doing business and executives remain insulated, regulation feels performative.

History offers a warning here. In late imperial systems, regulatory and administrative elites often became self-referential, focused on stability over justice. Institutions endured; legitimacy did not.

Effective regulation depends not only on expertise, but on **distance, courage and consequence**. Without those, oversight becomes ritual rather than restraint.

Micro-Case: Financial Conduct Authority and Payment Protection Insurance

The PPI mis-selling scandal revealed regulatory failure through proximity, not incompetence. Banks routinely sold unsuitable insurance while regulators relied on assurances and incremental enforcement.

When redress finally arrived, over £38bn had been paid to consumers — a scale that exposed years of deferred intervention.

The lesson is clear: regulators lose authority when enforcement becomes cautious and reactive. Expertise without visible consequence breeds cynicism. Oversight that arrives late feels performative, not protective.

9. Technology and the Illusion of Control

One of the defining features of modern governance is faith in technocracy: the belief that complex problems can be solved through better systems, smarter data and more refined processes. Often this faith is justified. Technical competence matters.

But technocracy becomes dangerous when it displaces judgement.

Institutions under strain frequently respond by adding layers of procedure. Risk frameworks multiply. Metrics proliferate. Accountability is formalised into reporting lines and dashboards. Yet the core question—*is this fair, and does it feel legitimate?*—is left unanswered.

The illusion of control emerges when institutions mistake process for authority. Decisions are defended because they were reached "correctly," even when outcomes appear perverse. Public frustration is dismissed as ignorance of complexity.

This dynamic fuels resentment. People do not object to expertise; they object to being governed by systems that appear indifferent to lived reality.

History suggests that technocracy without legitimacy invites backlash. In Weimar Germany, economic and administrative expertise did not compensate for political detachment. In late Soviet systems, procedural competence coexisted with a profound loss of belief.

Modern democracies are not facing identical conditions, but the pattern is recognisable. Systems grow more complex as confidence wanes. Authority becomes managerial rather than moral.

10. When Systems Protect Themselves

The defining failure of strained institutions is not error, but **defensiveness**.

When challenged, systems often respond by closing ranks. Legal advice dominates. Communications strategies replace candour. Language becomes abstract. Responsibility is diffused.

This instinct is human and understandable. It is also corrosive.

Institutions regain trust not by asserting correctness, but by demonstrating accountability. They lose trust when they appear more concerned with avoiding blame than correcting harm.

Across the cases examined in this section—VAR, refereeing, regulation, technocracy—the same pattern recurs. Systems designed to serve the public gradually prioritise their own stability. Legitimacy becomes something to be managed rather than earned.

Historical evidence indicates that this is the moment when decline accelerates. Not because institutions collapse, but because they cease to persuade. Authority becomes performative. Compliance replaces consent.

The lesson is stark. Institutions that cannot explain themselves clearly, correct themselves honestly, and restrain themselves visibly will eventually be challenged—not by extremists alone, but by the reasonable centre withdrawing its trust.

That is how systems fail without collapsing. And it is how political anger becomes rational before it becomes radical.

Case Study: Post Office Horizon Scandal

The Post Office Horizon scandal exposed how institutions can fail catastrophically without formally collapsing. Over two decades, hundreds of sub-postmasters were wrongly accused of theft or fraud due to flaws in the Horizon IT system. Despite mounting evidence, the organisation defended the system rather than the people harmed by it.

The institutional response followed a familiar pattern: legalism over judgement, process over justice, and reputational protection over correction. Senior leaders insisted procedures had been followed, while individuals faced bankruptcy, imprisonment and public disgrace.

What ultimately shattered trust was not the original error, but institutional defensiveness. Warnings were ignored, whistleblowers marginalised, and accountability deferred. The system protected itself.

This case demonstrates how legitimacy drains when institutions prioritise self-preservation. Expertise and procedure remained intact, but moral authority collapsed. The scandal stands as a warning: systems that refuse to admit error eventually face far greater damage than those that correct themselves early.

Reference: UK Court of Appeal Judgments (2021–2023)

SECTION III

POPULISM IS A SYMPTOM

Public anger is not the threat; ignored injustice is.

11. The Populism Mistake

Few words in contemporary political discourse are used as loosely—or as defensively—as "populism". It has become a catch-all diagnosis for public anger, electoral volatility and declining trust. In doing so, it obscures more than it explains.

Populism is not, in itself, a cause. It is a response.

Past experience suggests that populist movements emerge when large sections of society conclude that existing institutions no longer represent them fairly. This conclusion is rarely reached lightly. It forms gradually, through repeated encounters with asymmetry: rules that appear flexible for some and rigid for others; burdens shared unevenly; accountability applied selectively.

When elites describe populism as irrational, they reveal a deeper misunderstanding. Anger does not become politically potent because it is loud, but because it is rooted in perceived injustice. Treating it as ignorance may be comforting; it is rarely effective.

The danger lies not in acknowledging grievance, but in ignoring its source. Where legitimacy erodes, alternatives will be sought.

History offers no examples where moralising public frustration restored trust.

Micro-Case: French Yellow Vests Protests

The Yellow Vest protests were triggered by fuel taxes but sustained by perceived elite detachment. Protesters objected less to policy than to being unheard.

Government explanations focused on climate logic and fiscal necessity. Protesters focused on fairness and recognition.

The disconnect illustrates how populist movements form: not through rejection of reason, but withdrawal of consent. When institutions explain without listening, legitimacy fractures.

12. Security, Credibility and Elite Anxiety

Elite anxiety often surfaces in moments of rhetorical overreach. Calls for unity are paired with warnings about extremism; appeals to stability coexist with suspicion of dissent. The language of responsibility is invoked defensively.

Recent debates around security, credibility and democratic resilience have exposed this tension. Leaders speak of threats to the system while appearing uncertain about the system's own standing. Concern for stability is genuine. The problem lies in how it is framed.

When public anger is treated primarily as a security risk rather than a legitimacy signal, mistrust deepens. Citizens hear not reassurance, but distance. They are reminded that their concerns are being managed, not addressed.

History confirms that this framing is counterproductive. Systems preserve themselves by persuading the centre, not by warning it. Authority is strengthened when leaders demonstrate understanding, restraint and fairness—not when they imply that dissent is dangerous by default.

Elite anxiety is understandable. But when it replaces self-examination, it accelerates the very instability it seeks to prevent.

13. Growth, Immigration and the Ratcliffe Paradox

Economic debates offer a particularly clear illustration of elite contradiction. Few concepts are invoked more frequently than "growth," and few are examined less honestly.

Calls for productivity, competitiveness and expansion often coexist with resistance to the social conditions that make growth possible. Business leaders advocate state support while opposing migration. Governments subsidise infrastructure while condemning labour mobility. The rhetoric of opportunity sits uneasily alongside policies of restriction.

The public notices.

The controversy surrounding immigration exposed this tension starkly. Arguments for public investment in regeneration were paired with language that alienated the very workforce such growth would require. (I call it the Radcliffe Paradox.) The contradiction was not merely rhetorical; it was structural.

Growth depends on people—their labour, skills and willingness to participate. When elites argue for expansion while disparaging those who make it possible, credibility collapses. Economic arguments lose force when moral coherence is absent.

Populism thrives in this gap. Not because economic reasoning is rejected, but because it is perceived as selective. Where elites demand flexibility from others while seeking protection for themselves, trust drains away.

Micro-Case: Ineos and Labour Mobility

Calls for industrial growth frequently coexist with hostility toward migration. The contradiction surfaced repeatedly in UK manufacturing debates, where businesses demanded expansion while opposing the labour mobility that enables it.

The public recognised the inconsistency. Growth rhetoric lost credibility because it appeared selective: benefits socialised upward, burdens resisted downward.

This paradox reinforces the chapter's claim: economic arguments fail when moral coherence is absent.

14. When Moralising Replaces Listening

One of the most corrosive elite habits is moralising dissent. Language hardens. Tone sharpens. Critics are described as misinformed, backward or dangerous. Complexity is acknowledged selectively.

This approach may consolidate in-group confidence. It rarely persuades beyond it.

Historical patterns show that moral superiority is a poor substitute for legitimacy. When elites speak *at* rather than *with* the public, they reinforce distance. Political debate becomes performative, not connective.

The irony is that moralising often emerges from insecurity rather than confidence. Leaders unsure of their authority reach for certainty of language. Institutions uncertain of consent assert values instead of rebuilding trust.

Listening, by contrast, is risky. It requires acknowledging uncomfortable truths and uneven outcomes. It demands humility. But it is also how legitimacy is restored.

Populism fills the space left by elite deafness. It promises recognition where institutions offer an explanation. History suggests that recognition matters more than reassurance.

15. Centrism Without Consent

Centrism is often presented as the politics of moderation, pragmatism and reason. In practice, it can become something else entirely: a managerial consensus detached from lived experience.

When centrism prioritises stability over fairness, it loses its moral anchor. Policies may be technically defensible and politically cautious, yet still fail to persuade. Consent cannot be assumed indefinitely.

The danger is not that centrism lacks ideas, but that it lacks connection. It governs through process, not participation. It values continuity more than legitimacy.

History offers warnings here, too. Political systems that drift into technocratic centrism often underestimate how thin their authority has become. They mistake the absence of revolt for the presence of trust.

Populist challenges emerge not because moderation has failed intellectually, but because it has failed relationally. Where people feel unheard, they seek voices that promise to listen—even if the promise proves hollow.

The lesson of this section is not to romanticise populism or dismiss centrism. It is to recognise that **legitimacy precedes ideology**. Without consent, even the most reasonable politics becomes fragile.

Populism is not the disease. It is the fever. Treating the symptom without addressing the cause has never worked for long.

Case Study: Brexit and the Hollowing of Consent

The Brexit referendum is often framed as a triumph of populism over reason. A more accurate reading is that it exposed a longstanding legitimacy deficit. For many voters, Brexit was less about EU policy and more about exclusion from decision-making systems perceived as distant, technocratic and unresponsive.

Decades of economic restructuring, uneven regional investment and elite consensus had produced growth without shared benefit. When concerns were raised, they were frequently met with moralising language or technical explanation rather than engagement.

The referendum offered recognition where institutions had not. The result reflected not ignorance, but withdrawal of consent. Crucially, the shock was not that people voted to leave, but that elites failed to anticipate how thin legitimacy had become.

Brexit illustrates the argument of this section: populism does not emerge in a vacuum. It fills the space left when institutions govern without persuasion.

Reference: Goodhart, D. The Road to Somewhere (2017)

SECTION IV

BELONGING, LOYALTY AND IDENTITY

Loyalty endures where people feel seen — and fractures where they do not.

16. Newcastle United and Local Legitimacy

Few institutions reveal the mechanics of belonging as clearly as football clubs. They are not simply entertainment businesses or sporting brands. They are repositories of memory, identity and local meaning. When they function well, they generate extraordinary loyalty. When they falter, the reaction is rarely indifference.

The long relationship between Newcastle United and its supporters offers a case study in legitimacy at a local level. Support has endured through prolonged failure, mismanagement and disappointment. That endurance is not irrational. It is rooted in identification rather than transaction.

For decades, supporters understood that success was uncertain. What they struggled to accept was detachment—ownership that treated the club as an asset rather than a community institution. The anger that accumulated during those years was not about losing matches alone. It was about perceived contempt for local meaning.

When legitimacy returned—imperfectly and cautiously—it did so through signals of seriousness, competence and respect. Investment mattered. So did tone. Fans did not expect miracles. They expected recognition.

This distinction is often lost in elite commentary. Loyalty is misread as indulgence; anger as entitlement. In reality, loyalty persists precisely because supporters believe something larger than immediate outcomes is at stake. Football exposes, in concentrated form, a truth about legitimacy that politics often obscures: **people remain committed when they feel seen**.

Case Study: Newcastle United Ownership and Local Legitimacy

Newcastle United demonstrates how legitimacy operates at a community level. Supporter loyalty endured years of failure under ownership perceived as detached and extractive. Fans tolerated poor results, but not contempt.

The subsequent shift in ownership and leadership did not immediately deliver trophies, but it restored something more fundamental: seriousness, competence and respect. Investment mattered, but so did tone, engagement and stability.

The response from supporters illustrates a key insight: loyalty is not transactional. It is conditional on recognition. When institutions acknowledge belonging, communities accept uncertainty and compromise.

This case mirrors broader political dynamics. Institutions that treat people as consumers misunderstand why loyalty persists — and why it collapses when taken for granted.

Reference: Brown, A. Fan Power (2008)

17. Fans as Stakeholders, Not Consumers

One of the most persistent errors in modern football governance is the reduction of communities to consumers. This logic has spread from markets into public life, reshaping how institutions understand their relationship with those they serve.

In football, the consequences are visible. Pricing structures, scheduling decisions and broadcasting priorities increasingly reflect global audiences rather than local supporters. Clubs speak the language of engagement while pursuing strategies that distance decision-making from those most invested.

This tension mirrors broader institutional trends. When citizens are treated as users rather than stakeholders, consent weakens. Choice replaces voice; satisfaction surveys replace participation.

Stakeholders, by contrast, expect explanation, accountability and continuity. They accept trade-offs when they are acknowledged. They resist being managed.

Historical trends imply that institutions which confuse consumption with belonging misjudge loyalty. Markets can tolerate exit; communities often cannot. When exit becomes the only response, legitimacy has already failed.

Football reminds us that governance is relational before it is transactional. Institutions that forget this lesson may grow larger, but they grow thinner.

Micro-Case: European Super League

The proposed European Super League collapsed not because of technical flaws, but legitimacy failure. Clubs framed the move as innovation; fans experienced it as exclusion.

Stakeholders were treated as customers, voice replaced by market logic. The backlash was immediate and decisive.

The episode confirms that institutions with deep civic roots cannot govern through transactions alone. Belonging demands participation, not explanation after the fact.

18. Why Elites Misread Loyalty

Elite culture tends to be mobile, professionalised and abstracted. Loyalty, by contrast, is local, historical and embodied. This difference in perspective produces persistent misunderstanding.

From the outside, loyalty can appear irrational. Why support institutions that disappoint? Why persist when outcomes are uncertain? Why resist change that promises efficiency?

From the inside, loyalty is neither blind nor naive. It is conditional, but the conditions are moral rather than transactional. Loyalty persists when institutions demonstrate care, respect and continuity. It collapses when they signal indifference.

Political elites often misread this dynamic. They interpret loyalty as tribalism or nostalgia. They underestimate its rational core: the desire for belonging in systems that increasingly feel remote.

Earlier records indicate that societies fracture when elites lose touch with this dimension of legitimacy. Centralised authority struggles to persuade without local grounding. Identity does not disappear when ignored; it hardens.

The resurgence of localism, nationalism and community politics is not simply reactionary. It reflects unmet needs for recognition and voice. Where institutions fail to provide these, alternatives emerge.

19. Sport As Civic Proxy

Sport frequently becomes political not because it seeks to be, but because it operates as a proxy for wider frustrations. Decisions about governance, ownership and fairness resonate beyond the pitch.

This is why controversies in sport provoke such intense reaction. They tap into deeper questions about authority, fairness and belonging. When fans protest against owners, regulators or governing bodies, they are often articulating concerns that extend far beyond sport.

The politicisation of sport is therefore not an aberration. It is a signal. Where civic participation feels constrained, symbolic arenas absorb pressure.

Elites often respond by insisting that sport should remain "above politics." Past experience suggests this is unrealistic. Institutions that carry public meaning cannot opt out of political consequences.

Rather than resisting this reality, systems would do better to learn from it. Sport reveals how legitimacy is built and lost in compressed form. It shows that transparency, accountability and respect are not abstract ideals, but practical necessities.

Micro-Case: FC Barcelona Governance Crisis

Barcelona's financial collapse revealed how civic institutions suffer when elite governance drifts. Debt was concealed, risk normalised, and accountability deferred under the banner of ambition.

Supporters absorbed the cost, while credibility collapsed.

The club's crisis mirrors political systems under strain: institutions endure symbolically while trust erodes materially. Sport becomes a proxy because it exposes governance failure in compressed form.

20. Loyalty as a Measure of Legitimacy

Loyalty is not unconditional. It is earned and renewed over time. When institutions interpret loyalty as guaranteed, they hasten its withdrawal.

The lesson of this section is not sentimental. It is analytical. Belonging operates as a trust system. Where trust is maintained, loyalty endures despite disappointment. Where trust is broken, success alone cannot repair it.

Political institutions face the same test. Voters tolerate compromise when they believe decision-makers act in good faith. They disengage when they sense contempt or detachment.

History seems to suggest that legitimacy is strongest where authority is grounded locally and exercised with restraint. Centralisation without recognition breeds resentment. Efficiency without empathy breeds resistance.

Football does not offer a blueprint for politics. But it offers a reminder. Institutions endure when they understand who they are for, and when those they serve believe that understanding is genuine.

SECTION V

TRUMP AND THE HOLLOW ESTABLISHMENT

Democracies fail not through ideology, but through conduct.

21. Power, Restraint and the Slow Weakening of Institutions

Modern political argument judges leaders by policy results. The architects of the United States Constitution judged them by their relationship to power.

Donald Trump's presidency is therefore best read as a constitutional stress test. The Founders assumed ambition, ego and faction. Their concern was not disagreement but concentration—authority pressing against its limits.

George Washington warned against personal loyalty supplanting public duty. His fear was corrosion: officials pressured, institutions disparaged, boundaries quietly redrawn.

John Adams defined the principle with precision: a government of laws, not of men. Courts, elections and administration were to stand above personality. Undermining their legitimacy—even rhetorically—weakens them long before any statute changes.

Thomas Jefferson tied republican government to informed citizens. Persistent hostility toward independent journalism or verifiable fact diminishes that foundation.

James Madison assumed power would expand if unrestrained. His solution was structural rivalry. Executive impatience with Congress, courts or federal limits would not have shocked him; it would have confirmed his premise.

Alexander Hamilton defended an energetic executive, but never an unaccountable one. Decisiveness severed from constraint was not strength. It was danger.

The Founders would not have measured a presidency primarily by legislative victories. They would have asked a narrower and more difficult question: were the guardrails strengthened or weakened?

Their Constitution was designed to contain forceful leaders—not to rely on their restraint.

22. The British Contrast

The United Kingdom operates differently. It rests less on codified barriers and more on convention, precedent and internalised limits. Parliamentary sovereignty, judicial independence and civil service neutrality function effectively provided those in power accept both the letter and the spirit of restraint.

Where the American system institutionalises distrust, the British system institutionalises trust.

That trust has been tested. Disputes over judicial authority, parliamentary procedure, regulatory independence and public broadcasting have revealed how much of Britain's settlement depends on voluntary compliance. Some conflicts reflect legitimate democratic contest. Others reflect impatience with constraint itself.

In a convention-based constitution, boundaries are rarely breached dramatically. They are adjusted gradually. The danger lies not in one confrontation, but in cumulative redefinition.

Fragile Mandate: Liz Truss

Liz Truss entered office with full constitutional authority. The machinery of government stood behind her. Cabinet appointed. Policy direction declared. Formal power was intact.

Modern legitimacy, however, is multi-layered. It rests upon party confidence, parliamentary stability, public trust and market credibility. In September 2022, the proposed "mini budget" triggered destabilisation across several of these domains simultaneously.

Financial markets reacted sharply. Sterling weakened. Borrowing costs rose. Political confidence deteriorated. Public approval declined further. Authority remained in technical terms, yet consent across critical constituencies was draining away.

The collapse was not rooted in scandal. It reflected perceived misjudgement and erosion of competence legitimacy. Without confidence from markets, party and public, tenure became unsustainable.

The personal consequences were immediate and enduring: the shortest-serving Prime Minister in modern British history, permanently associated with instability. Office existed; legitimacy did not endure.

This episode broadens the legitimacy thesis. Withdrawal need not follow ethical breach. It can follow perceived incapacity. In complex systems, legitimacy is distributed. When enough nodes retract consent simultaneously, formal power cannot compensate.

Fragile mandates fail not because authority disappears, but because the ecosystem sustaining it dissolves.

23. Elite Exceptionalism

The Jeffrey Epstein scandal exposed the same structural weakness from outside electoral politics. Its most corrosive effect was not solely criminality, but the perception that proximity to power delayed scrutiny.

In the United States, Epstein's connections fuelled suspicion that elite networks operate under softer rules. In Britain, associations involving Andrew Mountbatten-Windsor and questions surrounding figures such as Peter Mandelson deepened similar doubts. The lasting damage arose less from verdicts than from hesitation, defensiveness and the impression of insulation.

Institutions can withstand individual misconduct. They struggle to withstand perceived exemption.

When citizens suspect uneven standards, credibility erodes regardless of formal legality.

24. The Structural Lesson

Across these cases—the Trump presidency, Britain's constitutional strain, the Epstein affair—the common thread is architectural.

Democratic systems survive disagreement. They falter when limits become elastic at the apex.

Some constitutions codify restraint; others embed it culturally. Neither enforces itself. When leaders test boundaries faster than institutions can respond, the system does not collapse. It adjusts. And each adjustment lowers the threshold for the next.

Constitutional decline is rarely theatrical. It is incremental.

Oversight becomes obstruction.

Scrutiny becomes hostility.

Constraint becomes inconvenience.

Once that reframing settles, institutions remain standing—but altered.

The Founders understood this. They designed against ambition because they assumed it would persist. Britain relied more heavily on character and convention. Both approaches depend, ultimately, on a shared acceptance of limits.

When that acceptance weakens, the system is not shattered. It is hollowed.

And hollowed structures are hardest to repair precisely because they still appear intact.

SECTION VI

LEADERSHIP, RESTRAINT AND RENEWAL

Authority survives only when power accepts its limits.

25. Leadership Without Spectacle

Modern politics has developed a distorted understanding of leadership. Visibility is confused with authority; performance with competence; dominance with strength. Leaders are judged by volume rather than judgement.

Historical accounts reveal the opposite.

The most durable authority is exercised quietly. It relies on restraint, consistency and credibility rather than constant assertion. Leaders who endure are those who understand the limits of their power and signal those limits openly.

Spectacle may mobilise attention, but it rarely sustains trust. Institutions led by permanent performance become brittle. Every decision is framed as existential; every criticism as betrayal. Authority is consumed rather than accumulated.

Leadership without spectacle is not passive. It requires confidence—the confidence to act without theatrics, to explain without condescension, and to absorb criticism without retaliation. In periods of institutional strain, this quality becomes decisive.

26. Stability as Authority: The Eddie Howe Example

Sport again offers a compressed illustration of leadership under pressure. In recent years, football has become an unlikely reference point in debates about authority and restraint.

Howe's tenure at Newcastle United has not been defined by rhetoric or self-promotion. It has been marked by consistency, internal discipline and trust-building. Progress has not been linear. Results have fluctuated. Expectations have risen.

What has endured is credibility.

Supporters have been willing to tolerate setbacks because leadership has appeared coherent and serious. Decisions have been explained rather than disguised. Stability has been treated as an asset, not a liability.

This runs counter to contemporary elite instinct, which equates change with action and churn with ambition. History suggests that excessive turnover often signals insecurity rather than resolve.

Authority is strengthened when leaders are trusted to see beyond the immediate moment. Howe's example is not transferable wholesale to politics, but it illustrates a principle too often forgotten: **stability is itself a form of leadership**.

Case Study: Newcastle United – Eddie Howe and Quiet Authority

Eddie Howe's leadership at Newcastle United illustrates authority exercised without spectacle. Progress was incremental, expectations managed, and decisions explained rather than dramatised.

Supporters tolerated setbacks because leadership appeared coherent and credible. Stability itself became a source of authority.

The case underlines a core lesson of the book: legitimacy accumulates through restraint, not dominance. Quiet competence outlasts theatrical leadership.

Reference: Collins, J. Good to Great (2001)

27. Competence Is Not Character

Elite defence often rests on competence. Decisions are justified as technically correct, legally sound or economically necessary. These claims may be true. They are also insufficient.

History is clear on this point. Competence sustains systems only when paired with character. When technical ability is detached from moral judgement, authority weakens.

Institutions frequently promote skills while assuming character. This assumption is costly. Leaders who deliver results while bending norms create short-term success and long-term fragility.

Public trust depends less on brilliance than on fairness. People accept difficult decisions when they believe those making them are subject to the same standards. Where that belief collapses, competence becomes suspect.

The repeated failure to integrate character into elite selection and evaluation is not accidental. It reflects discomfort with judgement in cultures that prize neutrality and process. Yet neutrality without ethics is not impartiality; it is abdication.

Micro-Case: Volkswagen Emissions Scandal

Volkswagen's emissions scandal demonstrated how technical excellence can coexist with ethical failure. Engineers delivered performance; leadership tolerated deception.

The firm met specifications while violating trust. When exposed, the damage far exceeded financial penalties — credibility collapsed.

The case confirms the chapter's claim: competence without character creates systemic risk. Institutions fail not when skills are absent, but when judgement is sidelined.

Performance Without Integrity: Lance Armstrong

Lance Armstrong embodied competitive triumph: seven Tour de France victories, global endorsements and a foundation carrying moral symbolism beyond sport. Performance appeared to confer unquestioned legitimacy.

Yet legitimacy in sport depends not only on victory, but on adherence to shared rules. When systematic doping was exposed, the narrative inverted rapidly. Titles were stripped. Sponsors withdrew. Admiration converted into disillusionment.

The damage extended beyond commercial loss. Armstrong's identity fused athletic success with moral resilience. Once integrity was discredited, both dimensions collapsed simultaneously. The higher the pedestal, the sharper the descent.

This case exposes a recurring organisational error: equating outcomes with legitimacy. Delivery matters, but legitimacy depends equally on the integrity of the process. Results achieved through distortion may suppress scrutiny temporarily, yet they accumulate risk beneath the surface.

Performance theatre scales; so does exposure.

In leadership contexts, fabricated authority often rests on curated metrics, selective storytelling or short-term gains. While visible success continues, legitimacy appears intact. When examination intensifies, credibility disintegrates quickly.

Armstrong's trajectory demonstrates a core principle: legitimacy built on compromised foundations converts achievement into amplified disgrace. Without integrity, performance cannot sustain authority, and once exposed, the fall is reputationally permanent.

Charisma Without Governance: Adam Neumann

Adam Neumann built WeWork on narrative — community, reinvention and disruption of commercial property norms. Investors responded not only to financial metrics but to vision and charisma. Charismatic authority accelerated belief and compressed scepticism.

During expansion, narrative substituted for governance discipline. As the company prepared for public listing in 2019, scrutiny intensified. Financial disclosures revealed structural weaknesses and governance gaps. Confidence deteriorated rapidly. The IPO collapsed. Neumann resigned.

The reframing was swift: visionary founder became emblem of excess. Charisma amplified ascent; it amplified exposure.

This case reinforces a distinction central to your argument: inspiration is not institutional legitimacy. Markets may tolerate informality during growth phases, yet they withdraw confidence when governance appears misaligned with fiduciary responsibility.

Charisma can mobilise capital and talent. It cannot indefinitely substitute for structural legitimacy. Once external scrutiny hardens, narrative elasticity disappears.

In organisational contexts, leaders who rely primarily on personality, rhetoric or symbolism often mistake enthusiasm for consent. Legitimacy rests instead upon durable systems — transparency, governance and accountability.

Neumann's trajectory demonstrates that charisma without discipline produces volatility. Authority grounded in personality alone becomes inherently unstable once subjected to institutional examination.

28. Due Diligence, Judgement and Moral Risk

One of the most revealing elite failures is not corruption, but neglect. Due diligence is treated as a technical exercise rather than a moral one. Risk is quantified financially while ethical exposure is minimised or ignored.

History offers numerous examples of this blindness. Leaders elevated for their utility later expose institutions to reputational and moral damage that far outweighs their initial value. The cost is borne not by decision-makers, but by the organisations and publics they serve.

Effective leadership requires judgement—the capacity to ask not only *can we?* But *should we?* This question cannot be outsourced to a process alone.

Institutions that neglect moral risk in the pursuit of advantage create vulnerabilities that eventually surface. When they do, trust collapses rapidly. Defensive explanations rarely repair the damage.

Due diligence, properly understood, is not about eliminating risk. It is about recognising asymmetry and responsibility. Leaders who fail to do so gamble with the legitimacy they do not own.

The Cost of Defending Legitimacy: Sherron Watkins

In 2001, Sherron Watkins raised internal concerns at Enron regarding accounting irregularities. Her intervention did not initially secure protection or affirmation. Organisational culture resisted scrutiny. Silence would have appeared safer in the short term.

Whistleblowers occupy a paradoxical position. They defend institutional legitimacy while challenging powerful actors within it. The personal cost can involve professional turbulence, isolation and uncertainty.

Enron ultimately collapsed under the weight of its distortions. In retrospect, those who sought transparency are viewed differently from those who preserved silence. Yet at the moment of challenge, legitimacy defence rarely feels rewarded.

This case complicates the narrative. Legitimacy is not self-enforcing. It depends upon individual willing to absorb discomfort to preserve standards. Organisations often tolerate weak or compromised leadership because confronting it carries personal risk.

The asymmetry is structural: short-term safety versus long-term integrity.

Watkins' intervention illustrates that defending legitimacy may not protect the individual immediately, but it protects institutional truth. Silence, by contrast, compounds systemic failure.

Authority endures only where individuals are prepared to challenge its misuse, even when personal cost is significant.

Micro-Case: Carillion

Carillion passed technical audits while concealing fragility. Due diligence focused on contracts and cash flow, not sustainability or moral exposure.

When collapse came, costs were socialised — pensions lost, projects stalled, trust destroyed.

The failure illustrates the danger of treating due diligence as procedural rather than ethical. Moral risk ignored is merely delayed.

29. What Elites Must Relearn

The failures examined in this book are not primarily ideological. They are behavioural.

Elites across politics, business and institutions have drifted toward insulation, defensiveness and moral exception-making. This drift is often gradual and internally rationalised. It becomes visible only when trust has already thinned.

The historical record implies that renewal requires relearning basic truths:

- Authority is conditional, not inherent

- Legitimacy depends on symmetry, not assertion

- Restraint signals strength more reliably than dominance

- Accountability must be visible to be credible

These are not new insights. They are recurring ones.

The challenge is not knowledge, but willingness. Elites must accept that legitimacy cannot be managed indefinitely. It must be earned repeatedly, through behaviour that aligns power with responsibility.

Where this alignment is restored, institutions stabilise. Where it is not, decline accelerates—quietly at first, then decisively.

What follows is not a prescription, but a reflection…

History does not guarantee renewal. It only clarifies the conditions under which it has been possible before.

The Hollowing Cycle

The argument of this book can be summarised in a simple institutional pattern. Across different countries, industries and organisations, the same sequence repeatedly appears when authority begins to weaken.

Institutions rarely collapse suddenly. They hollow out gradually.

The process typically unfolds through five stages.

1. Status Buffers Scrutiny

Those at the top begin to experience softer accountability.

Reputation, influence or proximity to power alters how rules are applied. Behaviour that would attract immediate consequence elsewhere receives explanation, delay or discretion.

At first, the difference is subtle. Over time, it becomes visible.

2. Institutions Protect Proximity

Organisations instinctively defend those closest to authority.

Legal caution replaces moral judgement. Internal loyalty discourages criticism. Reputational protection becomes a priority.

The goal shifts from correcting errors to containing damage.

3. Process Replaces Judgement

Formal procedure expands.

Investigations, reviews, compliance systems and communications strategies multiply. These mechanisms are often technically correct, yet they displace a simpler question:

Was the behaviour acceptable?

Institutions increasingly defend decisions on procedural grounds rather than moral clarity.

4. Accountability Becomes Selective

Consequences begin to fall unevenly.

Frontline colleagues face sanction while senior figures retain protection. Responsibility disperses across committees, legal processes and technical explanations.

Rules continue to exist — but they apply asymmetrically.

5. Public Trust Withdraws

Citizens, employees and stakeholders begin to adjust their expectations.

They no longer assume fairness. They assume insulation.

Trust rarely disappears immediately. It drains gradually, replaced first by cynicism, then disengagement, and eventually anger.

The Consequence

Once this cycle takes hold, institutions may continue to function formally while legitimacy steadily weakens.

The danger is not collapse.

The danger is normalised asymmetry.

Where power appears insulated from the standards it enforces, consent thins. Where consent thins, stability becomes increasingly performative.

Reversing this process requires only one principle — but it is demanding:

standards must apply upward as well as downward.

Where they do, authority strengthens.

Where they do not, hollowing accelerates.

Conclusion

Restraint or Decline

The argument of this book can be reduced to one sentence:

Institutions endure only when power accepts limits.

Across every case examined — corporate collapse, regulatory failure, populist revolt, constitutional strain, football governance, executive overreach — the same pattern appears. Systems weaken not because they are challenged from below, but because they excuse behaviour at the top.

Exemption is cumulative.

Defensiveness compounds.

Trust drains incrementally.

The result is not a sudden catastrophe. It is something more corrosive: a steady normalisation of asymmetry.

Citizens begin to assume that status mitigates scrutiny.

Employees assume that hierarchy cushions consequence.

Voters assume that accountability is negotiable.

Once that assumption becomes widespread, legitimacy thins faster than law can compensate.

No constitution is strong enough to survive prolonged behavioural erosion.

No regulatory code is detailed enough to substitute for moral judgement.

No communications strategy can repair trust that has been visibly breached.

The lesson is neither nostalgic nor radical. It is historical.

Authority is conditional.

It is not secured by title, election, inheritance or expertise. It is secured by visible restraint — by leaders who submit themselves to the same standards they enforce.

Restraint is not weakness. It is institutional courage.

In every era where institutions renewed themselves, the turning point was behavioural, not procedural. Standards were reasserted. Accountability became symmetrical. Proximity stopped buffering the consequence.

The alternative is predictable.

Where elites treat criticism as hostility, dissent as ignorance, and scrutiny as persecution, they accelerate the hollowing they claim to fear. They mistake insulation for strength. They mistake stability for legitimacy. They mistake management for consent.

History is unsentimental about this pattern.

Republics rarely collapse in spectacle. They erode through accommodation — one defended exception at a time.

The choice is not between order and disruption. It is between restraint and decline.

The hollowing cycle described at the beginning and end of this book can be reversed — but only when power once again accepts limits.

If power is exercised under shared rules, institutions stabilise.

If it is exercised above them, they thin.

The future of democratic systems will not be determined by ideology alone. It will be determined by whether those entrusted with authority remember that they are custodians, not proprietors.

The standard is simple.

No exemptions.

No insulation.

No asymmetry.

Where that standard is upheld, legitimacy survives.

Where it is abandoned, decline is not a possibility. It is a timetable.

Author's Note

I write this not as a spectator, but as someone who has spent much of his working life inside large institutions.

I have seen organisations perform brilliantly under pressure. I have seen leaders act with quiet courage and accept responsibility when it would have been easier to deflect. I have also seen the opposite — defensiveness mistaken for strength, proximity confused with protection, and standards applied unevenly for the sake of convenience.

The difference between those two cultures is not talent. It is restraint.

In moments of institutional stress, the temptation to close ranks is powerful. It feels protective. It feels rational. It is often the beginning of decline.

The most impressive leaders I have worked with were not those who projected dominance, but those who understood that authority is borrowed — and must be returned intact. They knew that credibility, once compromised, is rarely restored by explanation alone.

This book was written out of concern, not cynicism. Institutions matter. They anchor stability, protect liberty, and organise collective life. Their erosion is not inevitable — but nor is their endurance guaranteed.

If there is a single principle that experience has reinforced, it is this:

Standards must travel upward as well as downward.

Where they do, trust strengthens.

Where they do not, hollowing begins.

Restraint is not a theoretical virtue. It is a practical safeguard.

And it is the responsibility of those closest to power to practise it first.

Appendix: References and Source Material

A. Power, Elites, Authority and Legitimacy

- The Power Elite – Foundational analysis of elite reproduction and institutional insulation.

- The Managerial Revolution – Early account of managerial power replacing ownership accountability.

- Elite Theory – Circulation of elites and decay of governing classes.

- Economy and Society – Authority, legitimacy, and bureaucratic rule.

- The Revolt of the Elites – Cultural and moral detachment of elites from society.

- Why Nations Fail – Extractive vs inclusive institutions and elite capture.

- The New Ruling Class – Technocratic elites and democratic erosion.

B. Corporate Governance, Boards and Executive Failure

- Enron – Systemic governance failure and performative leadership.

- Lehman Brothers – Risk blindness, groupthink, and elite immunity.

- Carillion – Board complacency and institutional denial.

- Wirecard – Regulatory capture and executive deception.

- Boeing – Safety erosion under financialised leadership culture.

Supporting sources:

- UK Financial Reporting Council – *The UK Corporate Governance Code*

- OECD – *Principles of Corporate Governance*

- Harvard Business Review – Board effectiveness and failure analyses

C. Leadership, Fabrication, and Performance Theatre

- Leadership BS – Critique of leadership myth-making.

- The Halo Effect – False causality in leadership narratives.

- Good to Great – Often misused retrospective leadership attribution.

- Power – How leaders actually gain and retain authority.

D. Organisational Culture, Ethics and Toxic Systems

- Volkswagen – Normalisation of deviance inside elite structures.

- Wells Fargo – Incentives, fear, and ethical collapse.

- Uber – Founder dominance and cultural breakdown.

Academic and practitioner sources:

- Schein, E. – *Organisational Culture and Leadership*

- Bazerman & Tenbrunsel – *Blind Spots*

- Ashforth & Anand – "The Normalisation of Corruption" (Academy of Management)

E. HR, Performance Management and Institutional Weakness

- CIPD – Research on performance management and organisational trust.

- General Electric – Rise and fall of forced ranking systems.

- Amazon – High-pressure management systems and attrition.

Supporting research:

- Pfeffer – *Dying for a Paycheck*

- Deloitte – Global Human Capital Trends

- McKinsey – Organisational health and leadership studies

F. Public Institutions, Accountability and Deference

- Post Office Horizon – Institutional denial and moral injury.

- BBC – Governance failures and cultural protectionism.

- UK National Audit Office – Reports on public sector accountability

- Institute for Government – Civil service governance analyses

G. Financialisaton, Incentives and Short-Termism

- The Value of Everything – Value extraction vs value creation.

- The Financialization of the Corporation – Executive incentives and hollowing out.

- Private Equity – Evidence on leverage, incentives, and governance trade-offs.

H. Methodological Notes

- Case studies draw on:

    o Parliamentary inquiries

    o Regulatory reports

    o Court judgements

    o Annual reports and investor disclosures

    o Peer-reviewed academic research

    o Reputable investigative journalism (FT, Economist, Guardian, NYT)

Further Reading

- The Power Elite
  The classic account of how elites form, protect themselves, and detach from those they govern.

- Why Nations Fail

  A powerful framework for understanding extractive institutions and elite capture.

- Leadership BS

  A sharp critique of leadership mythology, symbolism, and empty virtue signalling.

- The Revolt of the Elites

  A prescient examination of elite moral withdrawal and cultural separation.

- The Value of Everything

  A challenge to financialised notions of value and elite reward.

- Power

  An unsentimental explanation of how authority is actually acquired and maintained.

- Organisational Culture and Leadership

  Essential reading on how cultures form—and how leaders shape or distort them.

Author's Note on Sources

This book deliberately blends **academic theory**, **real-world corporate failure**, and **institutional behaviour**. The objective is not to moralise individual leaders, but to expose **structural patterns** that allow hollow authority to persist long after legitimacy has eroded.